I CHOOSE
to Be Respectful

I CHOOSE SERIES

ELIZABETH
ESTRADA

I CHOOSE
to Be Respectful

I
CHOOSE
SERIES

ELIZABETH ESTRADA

Gratitude grows from a simple concept.
It starts with the action of showing respect -
Respect for your friends and even your mentors,
Respect for your parents and your elders.

There are so many chances to show respect in your life.
When you look around, you'll realize the opportunities are rife.
When you're getting on the bus to go to school.
Greeting the bus driver should be a new rule.

27500

You must be quiet while they listen for humming.
They need to hear if a train is coming.
Show respect when entering a building.
It's easy to be calm and so fulfilling.

SCHOOL

The class furniture and supplies deserve respect, too.
When we misuse them, you can sure they feel blue.
School is a great place to show how respectful you can be.
Don't talk out of turn and be sure to let others speak.

While the teachers are talking, try to actively listen.
Teaching you skills and knowledge is their mission.
When you're in class and you're about to take a test,
Even when it's difficult, always give it your best.

Here's a respectful thing that you can do,
Hold the door for the person behind you!
When there's an elderly person struggling to cross the street,
It's okay to help them stay on their feet.

When you give respect to places, people, and things,
You'll earn your respectful angel wings.
During the day, you might find someone in need.
Respect is taking the opportunity to do a great deed.

It's not easy unpacking bags, boxes, and jars.
Ask if you can help by unloading groceries from the car.
You've practiced all week and it's time for the big game.
Don't hassle or call the other players names.

It's okay to cheer when you score a goal,
But be respectful and try to show some control.

Respect is something that you should always choose,
Whether you win, draw or even if you lose.
Always shake hands with players after the game,
It's called good sportsmanship when they do the same.

Don't forget to tell servers "please" and "thank you."
Those words are respectful and easy to do.
Pass the plate of food around when you are able.
Make sure there's some for everyone to share at the table.

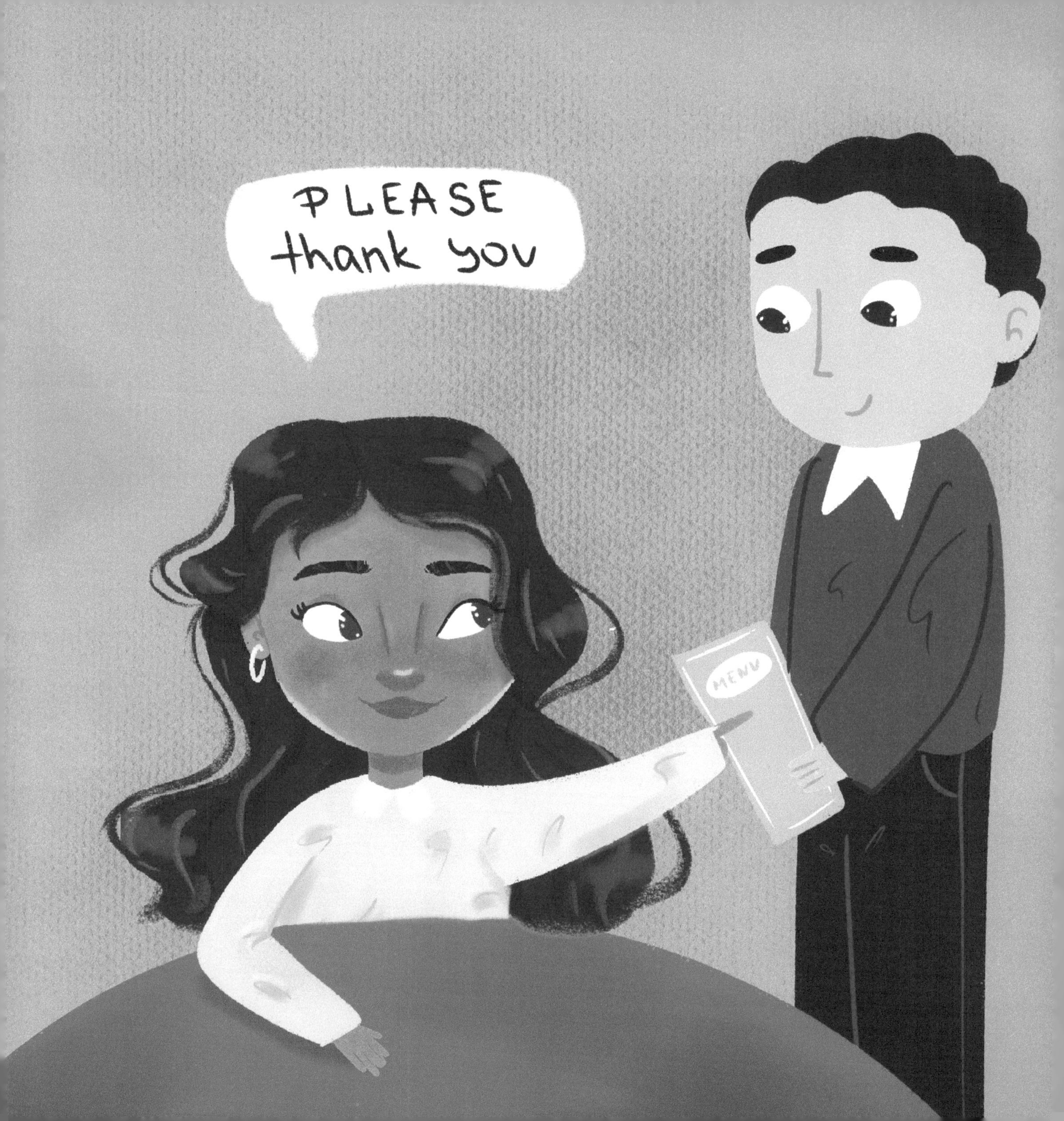
PLEASE
thank you
MENU

Sometimes we have to help around the house,
We shouldn't talk back to our parents or pout.
Scrub dishes, help fold the laundry, and clean the floors.
Be respectful to our mom and dad by doing our chores.

Showing respect is easy and can be quite fun.
You'll be proud when the day is done.
If there's only one thing that you can learn,
It's that respect is given when it is earned.

Dear Reader,

Thank you for reading my book. I hope you enjoyed a "I Choose to Be Respectful." I spent fifteen years piecing together resources and ideas to help young children cope with big emotions.

So please tell me what you liked and even what you disliked. What kind of emotion should be in my next book?   I love to receive messages from my readers. Please write to me at Elizabethestradainfo@gmail.com

I would also greatly appreciate it if you could review my book.

Your feedback matters a lot to me!

With love,
Elizabeth

Printed in the USA
CPSIA information can be obtained
at www.ICGtesting.com
LVHW071649301023
762357LV00044B/166